Wives

Memories *and Bedworth*

Published for the Working Lives Project by
Warwickshire Library and Information Service on behalf of Warwickshire County Council's Well Being Fund in association with Warwickshire Publications.

ISBN 978-1-871942-23-1

Book and CD designed by "Warwickshire Design2print."

Back cover photograph: View of Nuneaton taken from St Nicolas Parish Church, 2008. Courtesy of Warwickshire County Council.

CONTENTS

FOREWORD

Nuneaton and Bedworth have undergone major changes in the past 50 years and it occurred to me, whilst listening to conversations in a local pub, that a lot of the local industrial history could be lost if we didn't do something about it before people moved on to the big work places in the sky.

Listening to these stories made me realise that the best way to record this history was to get people to relate their stories about their working lives onto a tape recorder. I am very grateful that so many came forward to tell their story, and provide graphic details about the work they did, and others who supported the project with photographs and other information.

I would like to thank the Councillors of the Nuneaton and Bedworth Area Committee of Warwickshire County Council, for agreeing to supply the funding for this project, and also the Officers of that Committee for steering it through the initial stages.

Alison Clague was employed to develop the project and she embraced it with tremendous enthusiasm, and went to lengths over and above the call of duty to make it a success. Unfortunately Alison had to leave before the project was completed; however, we have been lucky enough to have had Louise Essex to see the project through to completion with equal dedication.

This book and the associated CD will give those that follow a sense of history, and hopefully a sense of pride, in the place they live, particularly as they can hear the words directly from those that did the jobs.

The real stars are those extraordinary people that took part in this project and gave it a real purpose.

Thank you to everyone involved.

Barry Longden
Chair
Nuneaton and Bedworth Area Committee, 2008

ACKNOWLEDGEMENTS

Working Lives was commissioned by Warwickshire County Council's Nuneaton and Bedworth Area Committee and funded by their Well Being Fund. The project was managed by Warwickshire County Council's Library and Information Service.

The Working Lives project team would like to thank everyone who made the project such a success. Special thanks must go to our many interviewees, who were so generous with their time, memories and cups of tea! Without their contributions we would not have this fantastic archive for future generations to enjoy. Special thanks should also go to Les Holmes who has volunteered his time throughout the project, conducting interviews, summarising them and contributing his local knowledge. Several people donated photographs and other material for inclusion in the project, for which we are very grateful.

Thanks also to Barry Longden, Andrea Buckley, Heather Shearer and Pam Williams at Nuneaton and Bedworth Area Office; Adrian Litvinoff for his continued interest and support; the staff of the Edward Street Day Centre; Toye, Kenning & Spencer for letting us visit and take photographs of their factory; Dr Rob Perks, Cynthia Brown and Julia Letts at the Oral History Society; Colin Hyde at East Midlands Oral History Archive, Bob Brolly and the team at BBC Coventry and Warwickshire; members of the Working Lives Reference Group; John Burton; Lynda Burton; Peter Lee; Alan Cook; Sheila Moore for giving us permission to include her poem; Yvonne Everitt; Lesley Kirkwood; Paul McIlroy; David Reed and all the staff at Nuneaton Library; Warwickshire County Record Office, Warwickshire County Museum and Nuneaton Museum and Art Gallery; Natasha King at Warwickshire design2print.

Working Lives Project Team, 2008

Working Lives

A Poem by Sheila Moore

Working! Working! All our lives
People at work, having to strive
To earn some money, to take the strain
Just like horses working in the rain.

Brickyards! Pits! Milk rounds! Quarries
You may have even driven a lorry
Or it might have been a horse and cart,
Whatever you did, you did take part.

We worked so hard to earn a few quid
It could be milk! coal or blue bricks,
Each job was hard, down a black hole
Tunnelling through like a mole.

Blood! Sweat! And tears, we laughed out loud
Nuneaton's workers can be proud
Stanley's! Judkins'! Co-op Milk rounds as well,
Sanderson's! Conner's! Courtauld's all fell

This poem's a tribute to our working lives
They have all gone now but memories we keep
It is all on record for all mankind
Talking about it, makes you laugh and weep.

Sheila Moore's mother and father
worked at Stanley's Brickyard and Sheila
grew up in a cottage at the entrance to
the works in Croft Road.

INTRODUCTION TO WORKING LIVES

Working Lives: the project

The aim of Working Lives was to record the memories of people from Nuneaton and Bedworth who had worked in the towns' numerous industries, focussing on brick and tile making, quarrying, textile production and engineering. Many former industrial sites have now been redeveloped and only traces of Nuneaton and Bedworth's industrial heritage remain intact. Recording the memories of the people who worked there was an important part of preserving this heritage for future generations.

What is oral history?

Oral history is simply the process of recording people's spoken memories so these experiences are preserved for the future. This type of personal and emotional information is often missing from industrial history. The hope is that some of the life and spark of the now disappeared industrial sites of Nuneaton and Bedworth are captured here.

Where

The focus was on people who lived and/or worked in the modern borough of Nuneaton and Bedworth. However, people's lives are not restricted by a neat geographical boundary. There was a lot of commuting to and from Nuneaton and Bedworth. Many people travelled to Hinckley to work in the hosiery factories or to Coventry's large engineering works. By 1931, 1200 workers a day were travelling to Coventry from Nuneaton to work, and by 1951 this figure had increased to over 9000. Many of our interviewees describe the large number of bicycles going to and fro, the busy railway stations and Midland Red buses full of people.

Who

We tried to interview a cross section of people who lived and/or worked in the modern borough of Nuneaton and Bedworth, from across the four industries, representing workers at different levels. We also worked with the Edward Street Day Centre in Nuneaton. These recordings include memories of people who had immigrated to the UK from East Africa of Indian and Pakistani descent. Many found work in the area's textile and engineering factories.

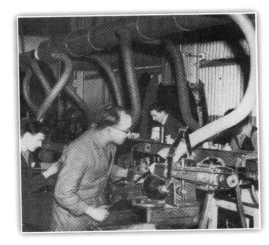

When

Working Lives captures a period of change in Nuneaton and Bedworth. The interviews cover a time period from the 1930's to the start of the 21st century, a period which included a World War and its aftermath, immigration from former British colonies and rapid changes in technology.

The interviews

This booklet and CD aim to give you an overall flavour of the interviews and some of the main themes contained within them. We recorded over 60 hours worth of interviews, so obviously there can only be a small sample here. These are edited extracts, but only edited in the sense that we have had to choose short sections, and remove some of the unnecessary repetition and 'ums and ers' that are barely noticeable when you are listening, but can be confusing for the reader when transcribed. Despite this, we hope that the unique individual voices speak to you clearly. We have tried not to alter any speaker's meaning or take any quote out of its intended context. Unfortunately space means that we could not include quotes from everyone we spoke to, but a list of all those who took part (and agreed for their names to be made public) can be found at the back of the book.

Listening

We hope these samples will encourage you to explore the website

www.warwickshire.gov.uk/workinglives

There are also learning resources on the website to encourage teachers to use the recordings in lessons. By putting the memories online we hope that we can reach people with an interest in the history of Nuneaton and Bedworth no matter where they live.

Working Lives Project Team

Nuneaton and Bedworth's industries were initially based on its natural resources of coal, clay and stone. New industry arrived in the form of ribbon weaving in the 17th century, and in the 20th century engineering became a significant part of the industrial landscape.

Ribbon weaving at Toye, Kenning & Spencer, 2008. Courtesy of Warwickshire Library and Information Service.

INDUSTRY OF NUNEATON & BEDWORTH

Well-connected by the canal system from the late 1700's and later the rail and road networks, Nuneaton and Bedworth's central position meant that the towns were well-placed to move their products around the country. The influence of surrounding areas was also felt; Nuneaton and Bedworth lie only a few miles

north of Coventry, and both ribbon weaving and engineering had spread from this industrial city. The proximity of the Leicestershire border also meant that many people travelled to lucrative work in the hosiery factories.

The nineteenth century saw rapid growth of Nuneaton as a town. The scale of industry increased as

the factory system arrived, and in Nuneaton and Bedworth this started to change the formerly rural landscape into one dotted with chimneys and imposing factory buildings. The population grew as a result of this and new houses were built from the thousands of bricks produced nearby.

During the Second World War there was a new addition to the towns' selection of industries. The bombardment of Coventry meant that engineering factories started to relocate to Nuneaton and Bedworth, including Clarkson's and Sterling Metals. The post-war period was a time for rebuilding the country and the brickworks and engineering works of Nuneaton and Bedworth rose to the challenge.

"It was chock bang full of factories. You could walk out of one and into another … it was just full of factories, full of work…"

Josie Stevens

Lister's factory on Attleborough Road in 1979. The factory was empty and in the course of demolition. Courtesy of Warwickshire County Record Office.

"When I was growing up there was the mining, there was the brickyards, there was the quarries, then there was the factories, like Conners the box factory and the Reliable textile factory and Hall and Phillips' the hat factory, all them they were there. They've all gone now. Courtaulds, they're all gone now."

Arthur Brittain

The 1951 Festival of Britain was a celebration of British design and manufacture. Nuneaton held an exhibition showcasing the wide range of industries within its boundaries. The booklet opposite claims Nuneaton was the 'Hub of Industrial Britain', quite a self-assured boast. Nuneaton's central geographical position and its diversity of industry meant that the mood was one of confidence for the future. There is no sense that less than 50 years later almost all of the major industries mentioned would be gone.

A pamphlet from 1973 continues to stress the diversity of local industries, with descriptions of 56 'sizable or unique' companies, while acknowledging that coal mine closures meant that new employment opportunities had to be identified.

The interviews reflect this diversity and abundance of industry.

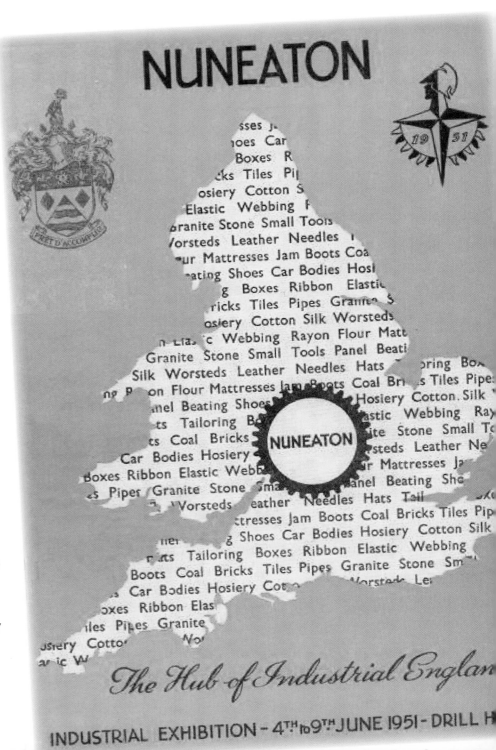

NUNEATON

NUNEATON

The Hub of Industrial England

INDUSTRIAL EXHIBITION - 4TH to 9TH JUNE 1951 - DRILL H

Industries in decline

"Even now when I walk up Bracebridge Street and when I take my children to the park behind where the factory was, I can still visualise where everything was. I can visualise which part of the section I used to work on where the actual houses are standing at the moment, where the loading bay was, where the offices were, where the canteen was. So it's really difficult sometimes to walk past and not feel that I belonged here at some point in my life."

Farida Sheikh

The site of Abbey Hosiery in Bracebridge Street, 2008. Courtesy of Warwickshire Library and Information Service.

View of Marlborough Road looking towards the Courtaulds site, 2008. Courtesy of Warwickshire Library and Information Service.

In the 1960's, the brick and tile industry had already started to wane, but the other main industries in the area continued until the effects of overseas competition and the decline of the British car industry were felt in the 1980's.

A report produced in 1988 for the Borough Council shows that manufacturing was starting to be replaced by service industries. Distribution and warehousing became, and remain an important part of the local industrial landscape. Many industrial sites have now been redeveloped and only traces of Nuneaton and Bedworth's industrial buildings remain.

The interviews reveal a real pride in the quality and range of work that was produced in Nuneaton and Bedworth. Sometimes a sense of frustration surfaces at the loss of skilled work and a bewilderment at the change from manufacturing to service industries. This often leads to the question 'What do we actually make now?'.

Courtaulds Medical Centre, Marlborough Road, (now Old Mill Surgery) 2008. Courtesy of Warwickshire Library and Information Service.

"But anybody today who's got an easy job must be lucky. Cause in them days it was like brickyards, pits all round here, Sterling Metals, in them days they were all heavy jobs."

Roy Jennings

TEXTILES

The textile industry in the second half of the twentieth century in Nuneaton and Bedworth was varied. It included traditional ribbon weaving, elastic webbing and narrow weaving, yarn processing at Courtauld's, hosiery factories, garment making, hatting and production of leather goods.

The textile industry had its roots in the seventeenth century. Huguenot ribbon weavers had settled in Coventry, which became a centre for silk weaving. This gradually spread the few miles north to Bedworth, Bulkington and Nuneaton. This was a domestic industry; weavers living in cottages with upstairs workshops known as 'topshops' which had large windows to let in the maximum amount of light. The whole family would have been involved in the work. In "Scenes of Clerical Life", George Eliot describes the town of Milby (based on Nuneaton) as *'a dingy looking town with a strong smell of tanning up one street and a great shaking of handlooms up another.'*

Ted Veasey, local historian, notes that by 1851 almost half of the working population of Nuneaton was employed in the silk ribbon industry and almost half of those were women. Women continued to be a major part of the workforce in the textile industry into the twentieth century.

**Courtaulds Ltd 1960's.
Courtesy of Warwickshire Library and Information Service.**

The factory system eventually arrived, with the first steam mill recorded in Attleborough in 1830. When the ribbon weaving industry collapsed in the 1860's after the removal of duty on imported silk ribbon, it left a workforce skilled in textile production ready to work in the new mills. There was a cluster of factories in Attleborough including a webbing factory on the Green, and Anker Mill on Attleborough Road. Anker Mill was originally set up as a cotton mill, but was later bought by Fielding and Johnson Ltd and converted to a worsted yarn factory.

"Noise, oh dear. You've got to bear in mind that the mules were backwards and forwards, backwards and forwards like a train. And the spinning, the bobbins were going round at a heck of a bat, up and down bang…all that was going through your head. You'd got a continuous headache, you'd have hearing problems…"

Alan Green

"I went to Lister's at Attleborough and I used to work in the dye sheds there, doing the dyed silks…and if there was no work for that I used to have to go in what they called the hand backing of the Lister's rugs…That was hard work. You used to cut all your hands with the twine…very thick twine. You had to put plasters all down your hand to stop you from cutting your hand…And then from there I went to Fielding and Johnson's and I just went as a reeler and creeler there. You used to put the six bobbins on the machine on to one bobbin to make the wool."

**Anonymous
female worker**

"I started off as a bobbin boy, that was in the mule room with the foreman whose name was Bert Sheldon… And what we used to do wait till the chaps had took all the work off the machine, put it in the basket, we used to take it down, get it weighed, come back, cleaning, fetching bobbins, taking bobbins…Then I went to work with a chap called Derek Warren…used to do all the maintenance on the machines, changed the wheels, changed the belts, altered the twist on the machines and then I went to college in Leicester…then I moved on to weaving."*

Alan Green

Alan Green

Marlborough Road, the gateway to Courtaulds Ltd still stands. The site is now a housing development. Courtesy of Warwickshire Library and Information Service.

Sharifa Khalifa worked for Courtaulds in the winding department and later in quality control.

Courtaulds specialised in the production of man-made yarns, and had a large factory in Coventry. In 1921 a large processing plant was opened in Nuneaton and immediately became a local landmark. The imposing red brick factory with its clock tower, parquet floors and associated buildings was on Marlborough Road. Over a thousand workers were employed over its four floors. Although the main factory has been demolished, you can still see the gateway, canteen and medical block today.

"I look after 62 spindles on it and working on two machines opposite each other…about 2 and a half pounds thread was going on it (the bobbin) so we can take it out and put another one on there."
Sharifa Khalifa

Courtaulds Ltd Courtesy of Warwickshire County Record Office.

Weaving

"Well I worked there until I got married, that was till I was twenty one. Then I went to Lister's for about nine month…It were better money at Lister's you know when you got married and that. But I never liked Lister's - it were filthy, filthy, fluffy, well you know covered in fluff you were… If you put your cup of tea down there'd always be fluff on top! "

Josie Stevens

Josie Stevens worked in various textile mills in Attleborough, including Lester and Harris and Lister Co Ltd, eventually becoming a quality controller at Courtaulds.

Josie Stevens working at a loom at Lester and Harris, early 1970's. Courtesy of Josie Stevens.

"Well, I went straight into the factory on Attleborough Green, Lester and Harris's weaving factory…They put me on with this old weaver, you know. But coming from school and then going in a factory, I mean what did we work? We worked from eight till six then, you know. And oh and it seemed endless and endless the days. And course they were ever so strict, you know, you couldn't go off talking to anybody, you know. But she were good, she trained me well for about six weeks I think and then when they gave me my own machines oh it were great you know, the bee's knees, you know, me own looms it were lovely. "
Josie Stevens

A company newsletter from 1970 shows new looms at Lester and Harris's Attleborough factory. Courtesy of Warwickshire Library and Information Service.

"Textiles has always been a low wage. But one thing about textile work, you was very rarely out of work. I never lost a day's work…all my life and that's in about 50 years in the weaving trade."

Joe Craner

"I went to Franklin's in Much Park Street, Coventry…And they moved to Nuneaton where Slingsby's used to be, Seymour Road, and I worked there for several years… Made labels, navy cap ribbons, all different types of weaving…all on the Jacquard…Franklin's had started one of the first high speed machine…they got one made by Wilkinson's in Paynes Lane (Coventry)…They had about twelve of those over at Nuneaton. I set all those up for them…and that was the first beginning to speed things up. …Of course the Jacquard loom as well they had different number of shuttles…tiers they used to call them…six were the highest number of shuttles we had. Six tiers that's making six different colours in the one label say.

The Jacquard had holes in the card and the needles went through the holes in the card and picked a hook up that picked the threads up at the bottom. "
Joe Craner

Toye, Kenning & Spencer in Bedworth is the last remaining weaving factory in the area. They still weave ribbons and use wooden Jacquard looms. Their specialised work, producing religious, military and Masonic regalia, has helped ensure their survival into the twenty-first century.

Joe Craner worked as a technician in the ribbon weaving industry. He started at Grant's in Coventry, later moving to Franklin's (in Coventry and then Nuneaton) and then maintained the looms at Toye, Kenning & Spencer in Bedworth for many years.

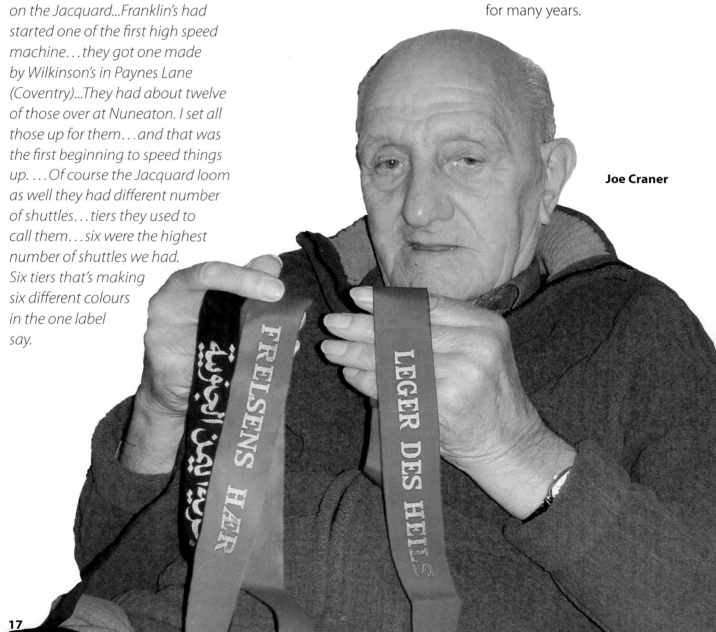

Joe Craner

A Jacquard loom in operation at Toye, Kenning & Spencer, 2008.
Courtesy of Warwickshire Library and Information Service.

Avis Keal worked at Toye, Kenning & Spencer in the 1940's, and can remember the Bedworth factory opening.

"They got bombed out with the Blitz and...they brought the firm… and brought quite a few of the girls that worked there they came with them… from Coventry…"

Toye, Kenning & Spencer's factory on Newtown Road, Bedworth, 2008. Courtesy of Warwickshire Library and Information Service.

Margaret Dewis worked as a supervisor or foremistress at Toye, Kenning & Spencer in the 1970's and 80's.

Margaret Dewis in the workroom at Toye, Kenning & Spencer, 1980's. Courtesy of Margaret Dewis.

She describes the high standard of work that was expected there:

"You went on simple things for a start, just to get the hang of putting lace on to ribbons and things like that…. At Kenning's though you never ever had what you call seconds...Everything went through as the best…It was a good policy. All the girls were very good.

The hand embroiderers worked on material stretched on frames. They used to fill the frame up with the work that I give them and once they had done everything they would cut everything out and put it in the bag with the ticket and it was all done, all checked. We never had many girls that used to have much time off. Obviously it wasn't very strenuous work but being over the frames and sewing all day obviously your eyes got tired, and on the machines. You were glad enough when 5 o'clock was there."
Margaret Dewis

Back L-R, Margaret Parker, Cynthia Kimberley,
Front L-R Janet Kinrade, Julie Watts holding a hand embroidered drum drape made at Toye, Kenning & Spencer.
Courtesy of Margaret Dewis.

"You kept a book…when you were actually on the machine you made your own notes, what lace went on what ribbon and that sort of thing."

Margaret Dewis

Sewing machinists at work at Toye, Kenning & Spencer, 2008. Coutesy of Warwickshire Library and Information Service.

The embroiderers and machinists were paid by piece work.
"You got a price for everything… everything was piecework and if we didn't think we were paying them enough I'd go down to have a word with Brian (Golder, manager) and say 'I don't think this is enough for this, what do you think?' And we'd work together and if we thought they needed some more, he'd give them some. He was very fair."
Margaret Dewis

A page from Margaret Dewis's work book.

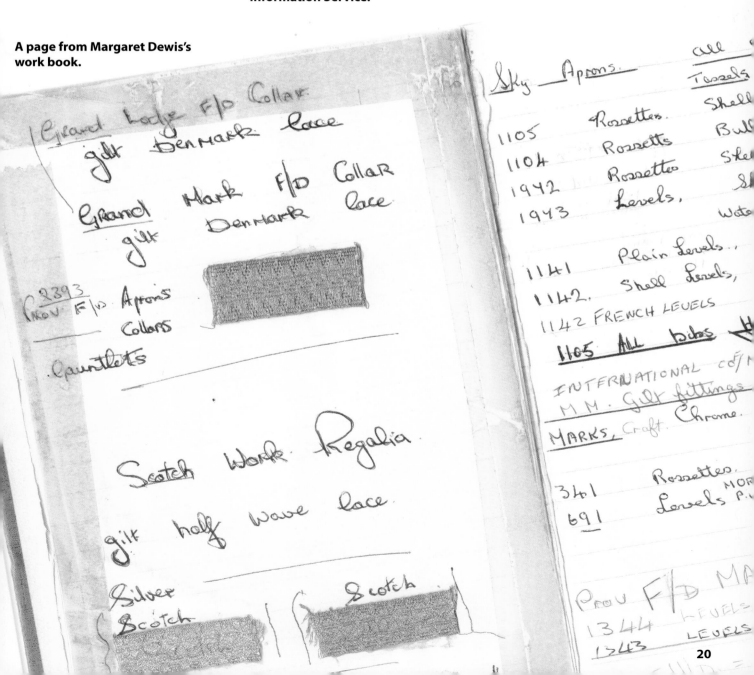

Hosiery

Hosiery was a major industry in nearby Leicestershire, but in Nuneaton and Bedworth there were also companies producing stocking-knit articles like baby clothes and underwear. Abbey Hosiery was a major employer in Nuneaton until the 1990's. It supplied Marks and Spencer until they transferred much of their manufacturing overseas. In 1988 it was recorded as being the largest private employer in the Borough with 1190 employees.

Farida Sheikh worked at Abbey Hosiery when she left school in the late 1980's.

"Everybody was split up into small teams, because boxer shorts weren't the only things the actual factory made. We made all sorts of garments from cardigans to T-shirts to long johns to boxer shorts, briefs…The factory consisted of six to eight hundred people….

Friday was the best day because it was pay day on a Friday and everybody used to finish round about quarter to twelve and we used to get our pay packets at ten to twelve…and on a Friday when we left the Bracebridge Street site all you can see through the doors at midday was loads and loads of employees walking out. And there was just a buzz…"
Farida Sheikh

Farida Sheikh

"But as soon as I moved into my house, I realised that I have to make sure that children are at school on time, they come home, I want to be there, so I started working at home. And it was hard. I used to have an overlocking machine and a lockstitching machine. I would jump from one machine to the other…That was my livelihood I didn't even think anything of it. My house was full of machines…And my children were young. I used to start working as soon as they go to school, I finished cooking…You have to make babygros… it takes you a whole hour to do a dozen, little toes, and everything, collars, little cuffs. And at the end of that, 90 pence an hour it would turn out to be… And I am particular in what I do, so I didn't care if I earned a little bit less but I wanted to produce perfect work."

Anonymous outworker

Mrs Zainub Kapadia worked as an outworker in Nuneaton.

But not everybody in the textile industry worked in a factory. Outworkers would have boxes of work delivered to their homes to be completed, fitting in the work around looking after their families.

Mrs Zainub Kapadia worked for 22 years in the hosiery industry making a variety of different garments including anoraks, skirts, underwear and babygros. She worked in several local factories including High End Fashion and Abbey Hosiery Mills but also worked for a time at home so that she could care for her family. She enjoyed working at Abbey Hosiery where they made clothing for large companies like Marks and Spencer and the quality of the finish was important.

Garment making

Nuneaton had two companies that specialised in making tailored clothing, the Reliable Clothing Company in York Street and Hart and Levy in Central Avenue.

"You'd got your stool, your machine…and you'd got this little bit of space that was yours, put your coat down under the belt…toffee papers and things on the floor…They were happy days actually. I don't think I've ever worked anywhere that I was as happy as I was there… Phyllis Grey…she taught us to use the machines and how to clean them and sew a straight line. I mean, you had to do a straight line down a trouser leg!

They were doing a lot of raincoats, these trench coats, gabardine macs and things…I can remember once we had a, we had a consignment of naval overcoats, and my friend she was on the sleeves. I was on the pockets and she was on the, putting the sleeves in…Well, she'd got it all mixed … And then the old chap that used to be the examiner come running round and he said 'Who's putting the sleeves in?' and she says, 'I am' he said, 'Well don't put no more in'. So, he says, 'Come and have a look what you've done.' And you know how you see a coat when it's on a hanger it's been pressed and then all the sleeves are there on and they're sort of curved a little bit. Well, she'd put that one in that arm and that one in that arm and they were all going backwards. He said, 'It's sailors you've got to fit them for, not penguins!' And we had to sit for days unpicking all these sleeves, you know all the stitches and get all the sleeves out and they had to be turned round, re-pressed. That was funny at the time, although she didn't think so. She was in tears.

Bill Strip…He used to cut out…I don't mean one thing at a time. There used to be a big pile of material and then these great big shears and he used to have to cut the garments out."

Eve Everitt

Eve Everitt started at Hart and Levy during the Second World War.

"The wages at the Reliable, they were like little tins, lower one side than the other. The receipts used to go to the foreman with the wages of each person who worked for them and he give them out to the people and then as soon as the windows went up…they used to come and queue up and they used to bring this slip and you used to tip this money out into their hands. Because you do realise that it would only be shillings, there wouldn't be a pound in it."

Angela Woodcock

Angela Woodcock worked in the office of the Reliable Clothing Company in the late 1930's until she was transferred to Dunlop Rim and Wheel by the Labour Exchange during the Second World War. Her job included typing labels and paying the wages.

Angela Woodcock

Hatting

Fred Arkinstall

"I was fourteen when I started at Hall and Phillips… But I didn't start my apprenticeship until I was sixteen… And I'm a fully fledged journeyman hatter, felt hat finisher."

Fred Arkinstall

Fred Arkinstall was the last person to finish an apprenticeship in the felt hat finishing department of Hall and Phillips' hat factory at Abbey Green.

"Hats were generally all handcrafted…It was bell-shaped when a felt-hat finisher got it and it was pulled over blocks to get the general shape into them and manipulated by hand. It was all softened with glasspaper and velour, sponges and things like that to get the finishing state…We made all sorts of hats, we made the Anthony Eden hat, bowler hat, trilbies, fez hats, ladies' general things…"
Fred Arkinstall

Hall and Phillips' hat factory, Nuneaton, 1920's. Courtesy of Warwickshire Library and Information Service.

Wool and Leather

"My brother-in-law he was the labour officer there and he asked me to come and have a look around because he knew I was out of work…and it was an eye opener for me really because I was walking back into the eighteenth century as such. When you walked through that factory, at Wool and Leather, everything was done mostly by hand."

Ron Baldwin

Ron Baldwin

The Union Wool and Leather Company processed sheepskins and produced leather garments on its site in the centre of Nuneaton.
Ron Baldwin worked there after many years working as an engineer for Webster and Bennett. Just before the tannery closed, Ron took photographs of the factory and its workers.

Photographs courtesy of Ron Baldwin.

Checking the hides.

"The chappie that was the first aider he left through illness so I was asked if I would go on a course as a first aider, which I did. And I got the job… and the things that happened down there was horrific you can imagine. They are using knives and scissors and hands stuck in the machines and there was quite a lot of bad accidents down there."

Ron Baldwin

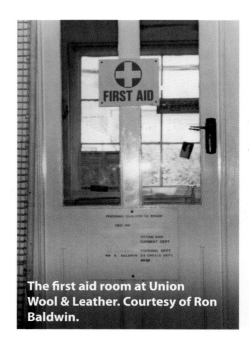
The first aid room at Union Wool & Leather. Courtesy of Ron Baldwin.

"Well you see you are dealing with sheepskins, raw sheepskins and the trouble down there was the rats. You opened the door to go in the warehouse and the floor moved and it was all all rats. But soon as you made a certain noise they'd go. But that amazed me where all those rats went to when the place was pulled down…I think in a way it was good for the town in some ways but it was bad for the people that's been there and that's all they could do, a job like that. But at the end of the day it cleaned the town up."
Ron Baldwin

The Union Wool and Leather Company closed in the mid-1980's and Sainsbury's supermarket now stands on the site.

Workers at the Union Wool and Leather Company shortly before it closed. Courtesy of Ron Baldwin.

QUARRYING

Stone and clay have all been extracted from the area for hundreds of years. Stone was quarried at Attleborough in earlier times, but in the period covered here, the quarries were concentrated around Tuttle Hill and Hartshill. Judkins', Boon's and Jee's quarries were all on Tuttle Hill. Judkins closed in 1996 and the quarry is now a landfill site, but 'Mount Jud' still dominates the landscape and can be seen from miles around.

Doug Watson's father was the manager of Charles Abell's quarry at Hartshill, and he kindly lent us many of the photographs he took as a young man.

Taken from Arrow Road showing Midland Quarry in the foreground and Mount Jud and Tuttle Hill in the background, 2007. Courtesy of Nuneaton Library and Information Service.

Doug Watson's father, Mr R Watson (third from left) with (l-r) Oscar Hardy, Harry 'Hicky' Hickenbotham, and another unnamed man below standing on a wooden elevator used to transport stone to the washer at Charles Abell's quarry at Hartshill. Courtesy of Doug Watson.

Shot Firing

"Cleaning out the quarry face with a shovel. When the machines had finished taking all the main body of stone out and you clean out all the loose rock and level it all off so that the drills could move in to drill the holes to take the explosive to blast the next lot down."

John Hopkins

John Hopkins

John Hopkins worked at Judkins' quarry. His father had started as an office boy and worked his way up to quarry manager, a role he had for many years. He wanted his son to follow in his footsteps and learn all aspects of quarry work. After 16 years, John eventually left quarrying to go and work in the car industry.

"Well the drillers would drill the holes into the quarry face, twenty, thirty foot deep…mainly they were put into the bottom, obviously you blow the bottom of the face out, the top will fall in on its own. They were about three inches in diameter the holes. And then we packed them with explosive, gelignite…depending on how much overburden there was you regulated the amount of explosive and then you packed the rest of the hole with clay…The shot-firer was a fella named Harry Hall and he had an assistant Tommy Taylor and they had been doing it since the year dot I think. So you just learnt from them as you went along…There weren't many mistakes…they usually got it pretty dead on every time. Because the object was just to lift the face up and drop it down again…and its own weight will break it up."

John Hopkins

"I was born on Tuttle Hill, overlooking the quarries…and I lived up there until about 1963… Mount Jud was always there. There was actually three quarries there… there was one quarry that was where the landfill site is now, the main part of it, that was the first Judkins' quarry. And then there used to be a road across the quarry approximately where Holly Stitches Road comes out there was a road across there to the fields and there was another quarry on the top side of that which was the one that I mainly worked at. And then next door to that there was another one called Boon's quarry which Judkins' took over in the late fifties. And then they made it all into one huge quarry then, blew the road up."

John Hopkins

Midland Quarry and group of quarrymen, Nuneaton, 1920's. Courtesy of Warwickshire County Record Office.

Crushing the Stone

"The primary crusher at Judkins' was always called Big Tom…that had to (be) kept going at all costs throughout the day…There were three sorts of stone at Judkins' – the quartzite, the diorite and the basalt. Plus on the outside there was a lot of volcanic rock."

John Hopkins

A promotional Judkins' matchbook, date unknown. Courtesy of Mick Russell.

Moving the Stone

"A lot of stone went to the railways, as ballast on the railway tracks. That was an ongoing thing, day after day after day. There was at least one lorry probably two loading the trucks all day every day…We tipped straight onto the railway sidings…Before that a lot of it went by barge and that was tipped straight into the barges on the canal. There was a wharf at Boon's and a wharf at Judkins', and there was also one at Mann-Abell's Hartshill, Jee's…"

John Hopkins

Mick Russell worked at Judkins' in the 1970's and 1980's. This line up of brand new trucks were delivered to Judkins in 1985. The owner drivers included; Barry Proctor, John Pemberton, Bomby Hales and Ted Kemp.

Courtesy of Mick Russell.

> **"About '63 or '64 was the first time we produced 2000 tons in a day at Judkins. That was a big milestone. Everything had been prepared carefully and there was plenty of stone and everything was running well. And we were going for the 2000 today. And we did it."**
>
> *John Hopkins*

Stone being loaded onto barges at Messrs. Charles Abell, Ltd Hartshill Quarries, c1910. Courtesy of Warwickshire Library and Information Service.

Draining the Quarry

"Of course [the spring water] drained into one big sump hole in the bottom and it was pumped out then used for washing the stone. If it was particularly dry then we had used to draw from the canal then. The old pumping place was stood for years along the canal just past where the bridge over the canal is…it was a wooden shed with a pipe running down from it…We had to have the canal dredged fairly regularly because even though the water was filtered quite a lot of sludge went into the canal. In fact I remember once up at Hartshill, a boatie coming running up playing hell up cause his boat had grounded – he couldn't get along the canal, we'd virtually filled it in!"

John Hopkins

A Dangerous Job

Quarrying was a dusty and dangerous job, which involved working with explosives. Ray Coles worked at Midland, Boon's and Jee's quarries in the 1950's and 1960's. He worked mainly as a driver, but also was involved in drilling, setting the detonators and operating the crusher.

"They used to pump a lot of water out from the quarry and everything into the sludge bed… It was just like a swamp, with all the sludge and everything. I mean, if you went in you'd never get out, no way. See if one of the chaps took bad on the crusher I used to go down…and then I'd got to go and help the bloke down the bottom and if they get jammed he's got a big iron bar…but it was a dangerous job if you ever slipped then you were gone, it'd just smash you all up."

Ray Coles

Shaking the Houses

Doug Watson's family lived literally on the edge of Charles Abell's quarry in Hartshill. When part of their garden fell into the quarry overnight, Doug recalls that workmen from the quarry came to fix the damage by simply moving the garden fence back a few feet. But it was not all dust and danger: *"We used to have to pump regular to keep the water levels down cause there were all springs running into the quarry. In fact when I worked at Judkins we used to have our own watercress beds there...It was perfectly pure water you could drink it...But I always remember that watercress, I've never tasted cress like it..."* **John Hopkins**

> ## "Cause the houses were up there, [we] used to go all the way round there and shout, 'Fire, fire'...then they just pressed the what's its name and it blows it all up. It used to shatter these houses. Just the vibration, you know a great big bang and it used to shatter the houses."

Ray Coles

The back fence of 21 Nuneaton Road, Hartshill, showing where the garden has collapsed into the quarry, late 1940's/early 1950's. Mount Abell is visible in the background.
Courtesy of Doug Watson.

BRICK & TILE

"It was all mostly pick and shovel, and a good pair of hands."

Roy Jennings

Clay had been used to make bricks, tiles and pottery in this area for hundreds of years. The local clay was used to make pottery in Roman times at Hartshill. Later, it was used to make bricks. Ted Veasey, in his history of Nuneaton, notes that a John Butterton was making bricks and tiles on Bar Green below Tuttle Hill in 1573, and many others followed.

The Brickyards

In the late 1800's, the completion of the railway and the arrival of two entrepreneurs, Reginald Stanley and James Knox, saw the development of brickmaking on an industrial scale in Stockingford. The products of Stanley's and Haunchwood Brick and Tile Co Ltd were used all over the country. Their bricks, tiles and terracotta work are visible throughout the town to this day.

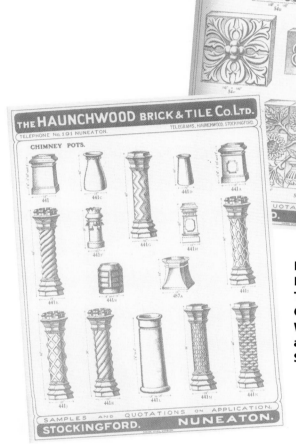

Illustrations from Haunchwood Brick & Tile Co Ltd catalogue. Courtesy of Warwickshire Library and Information Service.

The Haunchwood Brick and Tile Co Ltd was founded in 1878 by James Knox. There were three yards: the main works No.1 yard at Whittleford, No.2 yard at Heath End Road and No.3 yard at Bermuda.

Haunchwood Brick and Tile Co Ltd and the railway running alongside, Stockingford, early 1900's. Courtesy of Warwickshire County Record Office.

"I was born in Belle Vue, Stockingford. That's the top of Heath End Road in the little fourteen houses, industrial houses down there, made for pitmen and people who worked on the brickyards. My mother actually worked in the brickyard at one stage with other women on Four Yard, which was the glazed yard for sinks and material like bathroom sinks and the rest of it and the bigger sinks that we used in the domestic sense. And my father was a miner all his life practically. The second stage when he was made redundant at Griff Number Four, he then went to work at Stanley's brickyard which is located in the same area, by the Black Swan in Arbury Road. That was the original entrance to Stanley's Brickyard."

Edward Jephcote

Edward Jephcote has lived in Stockingford all his life and started work at Stanley's brickyard before the Second World War. His mother was one of the many women who also worked at the brickyards.

Illustrations from Haunchwood Brick & Tile Co Ltd catalogue. Courtesy of Warwickshire Library and Information Service.

Edward and his wife Margaret Jephcote

Sheila Moore also grew up in a brickyard house

"I lived at 303 Croft Road. It was a two up and a two down cottage. No electricity. We used to use oil lamps…We had a washhouse round the back where the washing was done between ours and

Croft Road, looking out of town, 2008. Courtesy of Warwickshire Library and Information Service.

next door neighbours, we used to share it. The toilets were about 30 yards away…Freezing cold when you used to go down there…When we used to go to our house we used to walk up the driveway to Stanley's brickyard which is where my mother and father used to work… My mother used to stack the bricks onto a large barrow and wheel them into the kiln…"

Sheila Moore

Reginald Stanley arrived in Nuneaton in 1867. He joined Stanley Brothers and started to expand the business using the fortune he had made in the American gold rush. Stanley Brothers Ltd eventually operated seven brickyards in Nuneaton as well as others in Coventry and Stoke-on-Trent and also two collieries. He also founded the Nuneaton Engineering Company, which developed coal mining and brickmaking machinery to speed up production.

The chimneys of these large brickyards dominated the skyline, their smoke filled the air and clay holes dotted the landscape. The Haunchwood site is now reverting to nature at Whittleford Park, although fragments of its products can still be glimpsed through the undergrowth.

Haunchwood Brick and Tile site; now Whittleford Park, 2008. Courtesy of the Bricks to Nature Project.

In the Clayhole

"When they were short down the clay hole, I went down there. And I knew where I'd sooner be – tippling, you know cause that was very hard work down there. Hand fill by shovel. And you're on all day long. You never had a minute until you had a break. Continuous bending your back, filling the tubs up, pushing them down to be clipped on to come back up to the mill. But as I say it was really hard work. Mind nearly all the work over there were hard work. And of course it was piecework, you kept going all day long because that mill wouldn't stop. They had to keep feeding that mill, and if that mill didn't have (clay) the foreman would want to know why."

Roy Jennings

Roy Jennings operated the tub tippler. Tubs on rails were attached to an endless rope haulage system to carry clay from the clay holes to the brickyard buildings. The tippler upended the tubs, tippling the clay onto a conveyor belt which took it to be processed and made into bricks or tiles.

Roy Jennings worked at Haunchwood Brick and Tile Co Ltd in the 1960's. He is pictured here at Whittleford Park, holding one of the brickwork's products.

Weighing the clay

"I got this job weighing the clay as they called it, in the brickyard. I'd got a little hut to myself and weighing scales and all that and books and everything. I used to have to weigh all the wagons, cause they used to have the clay come out the clay hole and they used to grind it in the pan and it used to come out in big clots like that and you used to cut it off and put it on the wagons and they used to have a horse and they used to pull the wagon on to the weigh scales. And I had to look out the window to see as they hadn't got the horse's foot on the scales to make it heavier. That were all the dodges like that!"

Arthur Brittain

Arthur Brittain worked at both Stanley Brothers and Haunchwood Brick and Tile Co Ltd.

Preparing the clay

"The first job I did at Stanley's was learn how to do the clay. It was sieved after the mill had ground the clay and its contents. It used to come up on a little elevator into two screens which I had to keep perfectly clean and…it sieved it and all the remnants went back down into the mill for regrinding. But I had to make sure there was sufficient going through the sieves at all times with a little wire brush and an ordinary brush to keep the place clean. A very dusty little job but I enjoyed it nevertheless. That was the beginning of, if you call it, my apprenticeship. Well I moved on to the ridge shed which makes ridges for the various roofs, you know the pitches and so on and the variety of stuff that Stanley's produced at that time. We used to have to run like the devil with our stuff and work really hard even as youngsters. So we were taught what work was about the hard way. I really enjoyed it because it was a physical job and I had some real good friends amongst them".
Edward Jephcote

Setting the Kiln

Setting was the process of stacking the bricks in the kiln ready for firing to bake them hard.
Here, Frank Alton sets a kiln at the National Coal Board's Ansley Hall Brick Works in Warwickshire, 1969.
Courtesy of Warwickshire County Record Office.

Opening the Kiln

Brick kilns would be left to fire over a number of days. Test bricks were used to show when the bricks were ready.

Peter Hornsby worked at Haunchwood Brick and Tile Co in the gang that set the bricks in the kilns and also as a brickie's labourer.

"On the top of the kilns they used to be little holes…where they used to put what they called, it's like a little brick with an hole, a set with an hole in, so they put the rod through it and they lifted it up and when that was cooked then they used to open the kiln. And when they used to open them then, well it was hot in there so you used to have no shirt on cause it was too hot."

Peter Hornsby

In the tunnels

"They used to have the kids about fourteen, that was their first job running up and down these flues, cause they used to be hot."

Arthur Brittain

A brick kiln on the Judkins' site. Courtesy of Nuneaton Library and Information Service.

Flues were tunnels that circulated heat throughout the drying sheds and the kilns. The flues needed maintaining and this was a job that the young workers used to have to do.

Chimneypots & Crinoline Ladies

"We used to get the clay, used to hurl it, the big blocks of clay, ready to make the chimney pots. One of my uncles used to do all the fancy chimneypots, used to make what they call crinoline ladies. Used to wheel them out on, you could hold two chimneypots…you had to be careful cause if you hit a bump the chimneypot would collapse. And then you used to set these inside the kiln, these were different types of kilns to the others."
Peter Hornsby

Sam Preston with the chimneypots he made at Haunchwood Brick & Tile Co Ltd. Courtesy of Geoff Edmunds/ Peter Lee.

Women Workers

"They (the women) worked at the back of the mill in that little place called the backhouse. That's where they used to make the tiles and the bullnose bricks and they were blues, and they used to be on the presses. They used to put the lump of clay in like that, which some of that were heavy, put it in and the press come down, they pulled the press down. Then when they pressed them they stacked them on trucks and they used to have a labourer wheeling them out to the drying sheds. But them women had heavy jobs as well. There's many women over there you used to see them wheeling barrows and clearing the deck where they were working and all that, so they had hard jobs as well. I say, I don't think there were many easy jobs over there."

Roy Jennings

Bull nose bricks from Stanley Brothers Ltd catalogue. Courtesy of Warwickshire Library and Information Service.

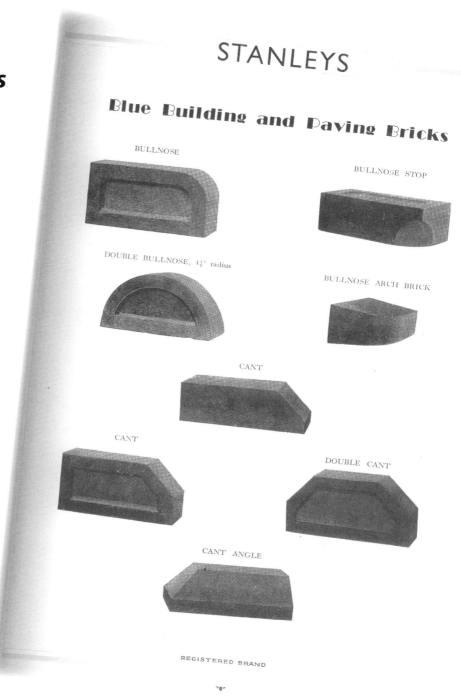

STANLEYS

Blue Building and Paving Bricks

BULLNOSE

BULLNOSE STOP

DOUBLE BULLNOSE, 4½" radius

BULLNOSE ARCH BRICK

CANT

CANT

DOUBLE CANT

CANT ANGLE

REGISTERED BRAND

ENGINEERING

Reginald Stanley founded the Nuneaton Engineering Company in 1889, which developed machinery for coal mining and brick making. But it was the Second World War that caused other large firms to relocate to Nuneaton and Bedworth, because they were bombed out of Coventry (as Clarkson's were in 1940). By 1951, engineering had become the largest employer in the area.

"I joined in 1958, Clarkson's in those days, in the early 60's, it was a buoyant company and they were beginning to expand down south and beginning to have subsidiaries. And it was a magic firm to work for, great team spirit. If you had a job with Clarkson's or the other was Sterling Metals, you were amongst the elite in town…It was really booming in the late 60's."

John Heathcote

John Heathcote

"Clarkson's made cutting tools, engineering cutting tools, milling machines, metal removal, basic bread and butter cutting tools that today I see forty years later still being used. They later expanded onto twist drills. The late Mr Frank Clarkson who founded the company, he invented a chuck to hold a cutter and it was a
universal chuck and it could do any operation on any machine. It was really a fantastic thing. We made lots of versions of cutting tools, we heat treated them to a certain metallurgical requirement so they would last for a long time, we later introduced different cobalt and things into the alloy so they would last even greater."

John Heathcote

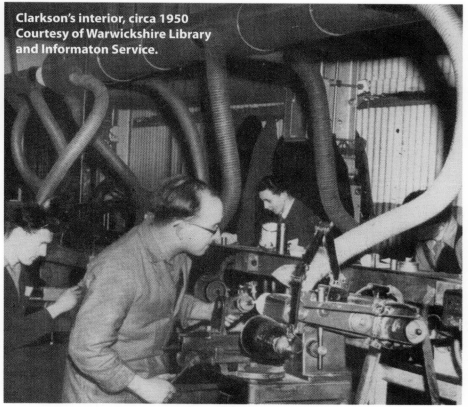

**Clarkson's interior, circa 1950
Courtesy of Warwickshire Library and Informaton Service.**

"The steel come in, it went first to the turning, then the milling, then the grinding, cutter grinding, heat treatment and out in the stores for sale…When it was dropped off the lorry as steel to when it was sold was a cycle time of thirteen weeks. It did shorten because the machinery changed…I think it come down to eight weeks in the finish."

John Smith

The site of Clarkson's in King Edward Road, 2008. Courtesy of Warwickshire Library and Information Service.

After over 50 years in Nuneaton the factory eventually closed down, leaving the remaining employees without pensions.

"The firm had been took over two or three times and the last people that bought it…it was underfunded so they were taking our pension money out to prop the firm up. That's why I haven't got a pension…I rode in down to work on this morning and I seen our manager standing at the door shaking his head more or less… And when I got in they told me the receivers had been brought in. That's the first we knew. So that was it. And then it finished in April 2001."

John Smith

Clarkson's factory. Courtesy of Warwickshire Library and Information Service.

Foundry & Sheet Metal Work

Sterling Metals moved to their large site on Gipsy Lane, Nuneaton during the Second World War. It was a foundry specialising in magnesium alloys and other types of casting.

Bill Baker started in magnesium light alloy casting at Sterling Metals and recalls the variety of parts that were made there, including part of Concord's nose cone and parts for the Mini car. He was made redundant but was offered his job back after 8 months, when he worked as part of a labour pool.

"There were 24 hour working on the Mini parts. Wagon after wagon coming out of the factory, they couldn't produce enough. Then all of a sudden all that stopped. I mean the reason it stopped was Maggie Thatcher come in and she said if anything's not making money it shut…Cause we was suppliers then it goes back to the suppliers and you've got to find something else then to replace what you've lost. And it just wasn't there, there were more places shutting...Then they started shipping complete foundries and factories to Poland and India and places like this so they were shutting us down and making 300 or 400 redundant…I mean when I started working there, there were 3200 worked there. When they shut it down there were less than 600.

You've got four sections. You've got Number 1 which I was in, then you've got Number 2 which was the fettling for Number 1, then you've got Number 3 were the die shop and Number 4 were the iron. But they all run different… the different environments, different working practices. They were all casting and making castings but it were a totally different way to doing it. So what affected the iron didn't affect us. So if the iron had a dispute we used to say let the iron sort it out.

I think it were only when it come down to redundancies that everybody were affected. You know we'd say we would sooner go on short time working than have redundancies because we know full well three months later they'll be setting back on… When we first started we thought you'd got a job for life but it never worked out that way."
Bill Baker

Bill Baker

"I suppose unless you worked there it would be a bit like hell I should think – it was hot, dusty, dirty. But then again people earned a living so it didn't bother them.

You can put a t-shirt on and in 10 minutes it'd be wet through. And you'd take it off, just hang it somewhere to dry and put another one on. And within 10 minutes that would be wet through but the other one would be bone dry, it would be like cardboard and it would be white where the salt from your sweat. So you'd just shake it and put that on. You'd got to be covered... On certain jobs used to be quarter of an hour on and quarter of an hour off so there would be 2 of you doing it...used to go outside then, cool down, have a drink... You couldn't do the job unless you were doing it like that. It were that hot you'd be passing out."

Bill Baker

Sterling Way, the site of Sterling Metals Ltd factory taken from Marston Lane, 2008. Courtesy of Warwickshire Library and Information Service.

Advertisement from 1951, Courtesy of Warwickshire Library and Information Serivce.

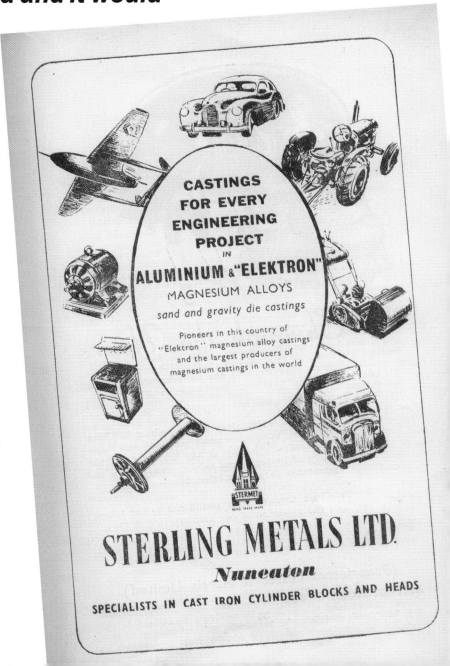

45

Dennis Lovatt worked at Sanderson Engineering at the Bullring in Nuneaton for twenty-two years, until 1973. An iron foundry and engineers, Sanderson's made replacement parts for local collieries and brickworks, following each job from start to finish turning, milling and welding. The company moved to a purpose built factory in Heath End Road in 1960.

Dennis Lovatt

"Safety was nothing then. I mean it were dangerous in the foundry as well… When they finished with the scrap they used to make them into ingots then and melt them down again and if the moulds were cold they'd blow up…No safety about then."

Dennis Lovatt

"I started…on the incendiary bombs and I were on a lathe. You know what my first wage were? Fifty pence. Aye, fifty pence… We used to work half past seven till half past five at night and we used to have to work Saturdays afternoons…and Sundays as well. And you know what my wage were? About four pound fifty a week, sometimes it were five pound for a full week…So the money weren't very good, not really no. And then I done all sorts of jobs there you see, I were on the lathe doing the tailfins…Then I were on the drilling putting the holes in for the tailfins to fit in…We used to have to pack the bombs up then in a box and send them up to Scotland to be filled with the incendiary stuff…"

Mary Spicer

Mary Spicer started work at Sterling Metals during the war. Staying on after the war, she was one of only a few women who worked there.

"I went into the buying department and finished up as a buyer... Then in the end I was the expense buyer for the wheel division. You know bits and pieces. In other words I didn't buy big machines but I bought the nuts and bolts for them."

Angela Woodcock

Angela Woodcock was one of the many people from Nuneaton and Bedworth who commuted to the large engineering factories in Coventry. She worked at the Dunlop Rim and Wheel factory in Foleshill. Starting off doing secretarial work, she eventually became a buyer.

Eric Byewater

Sheet metal working was an important industry in Nuneaton and Bedworth, supplying panels to the car and aircraft factories in Coventry.

Eric Byewater's father left Daimler and with nine colleagues decided to start up a company of their own. This was the Midland Sheet Metal Works. When Eric Byewater returned to Nuneaton after the war he started work there as a manager and eventually became a company director.

Geoff Elliott was a sheet metal worker specialising in wheeling panels for the car and aircraft manufacturing industries. Completing his apprenticeship at J.S. Chinn's in Exhall, Geoff worked in the trade in Nuneaton and Coventry. An active trade unionist, he was a shop steward for the National Union of Sheet Metal Workers and Coppersmiths and served as Branch President.

Geoff Elliott in 1950's. Courtesy of Geoff Elliott.

Tools of the Trade

"Every time you brought the tea round or at the end of the week, somebody would give you a tanner, somebody gave you a shilling, somebody gave you two bob. And that was to be kept and put into a tin…I can't remember how much I saved up, but it enabled me to go and buy my first lot of tools. 'Cause you had to buy your own tools. They supplied you with nothing. The only things they supplied you with were consumables, things that wore out. But anything else; your own hammers, your own hand weights, dollies, your own snips, everybody had to buy their own tool kit…I mean it was nothing to have 30 or 40 hammers, planishing hammers, blocking hammers …all different shapes and sizes, different weights. Three, four pairs of tin snips for different things."

Ian Cartwright,
Midland Sheet Metal Works

Ian Cartwright

48

Apprenticeship

"Men were very strict with you when you were an apprentice. If you didn't behave yourself they'd hit you, you know that type of thing, which today there don't seem so much discipline and it seems a bit more lax."

Geoff Elliott

For many apprentices some time at a technical college was necessary.

"Hated tech, I hated it. I used to catch the bus at the Nest, up Hilltop and get to Pool Meadow and decide toss up whether I went or not and then if it come round that way I'd do it, quite often catch the same bus back home and go. I hated it, I really detested that."
Geoff Elliott

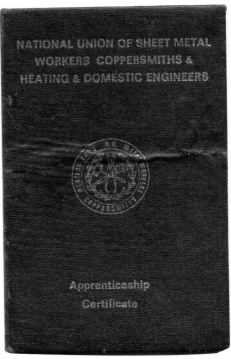

Ian Cartwright's apprenticeship papers. Coutesy of Ian Cartwright.

Apprenticeship Certificate

This is to Certify that

I Cartwright

has been enrolled as an Apprentice

SHEET METAL WORKER

Member of the *Coventry* BRANCH of the above Society on the *30 January* 19*70* and that he commenced his apprenticeship with the firm of *MIDLAND SHEET METAL CO.* on *30 JANUARY* 19*70* at the age of *16* years. and has undertaken to serve four years thereat, during which period he will diligently endeavour to aquire the skill and experience essential to the work of one of the oldest and most highly skilled crafts,

Signature of Apprentice..

In witness thereof we have attached the signature and affixed the Seal of the Society.

.... General Secretary

Date *30/1/70*

National Union of Sheet Metal Workers, Coppersmiths, Heating and Domestic Engineers

HEAD OFFICE:
75-77 WEST HEATH ROAD, HAMPSTEAD, LONDON, N.W.3

This Society will recognise any young man as a legitimate apprentice who has been supplied with one of these Apprentice Cards.

This Card is to the owner a Certificate of the Society's recognition of his apprenticeship and a guarantee to him that his workmates, members of this Society, will assist him to the utmost of their ability to become a competent workman, always provided he is in complete compliance with the Society's Rules.

This card must be returned to the Branch Secretary once a year for endorsement in spaces set out below. On completion of apprenticeship this Certificate is to be sent to the Society's Registered Office for final certification.

Initials

Branch Secretary's endorsement

This is to Certify that

Bro. *I Cartwright*

of *Coventry* Branch has completed his apprenticeship with the firm of

M *Midland Sheet Metal*

on the *30 January* 19*74*. and is a Skilled *Sheet Metal Worker* and a Section 1 member

In witness thereof my signature and the Seal of the Society.

.... General Secretary

Date *10/5/74*

Diversity of Industry

Engineering was not limited to large factories and workshops. Roy Dymock worked in a small subcontract tool room on Anker Street:

"At the time people wanted to be engineers. The car industry was really taking off, the Standard Motor Company…Morris Motors in Coventry, Alfred Herbert's which was the big machine tool company…I wanted to be a tool maker and I done an apprenticeship up Anker Street in Nuneaton at a company called S and F Engineering…the two owners were called Shepherd and Fitzgerald. And they had this little tool room at the top of Anker Street. At the back of it was Clarkson's…S and F Engineering would make anything. They made automatic machines for the Ministry of Defence…we even made a catafalque which is a machine which takes the coffin into the crematorium. And the main source of income for the company was packets of salt for Smiths Crisps …. And this machine that he invented filled these packets with salt then cut them off. And instead of selling the machine to Smiths he kept the machine, in fact he made about 20 of them…."
Roy Dymock

"During the course of fifty years ninety five percent of the sheet metal shops have gone. There's nothing left in the trade. Technology's eroded a lot of it but at the same time, when I was working two, three year ago, I was still wheeling, making and shaping and wheeling, hammering hand-pressed panels, hand-shaped panels for aircraft. That type of work is still done. It's a specialist job."

Geoff Elliott

Roy Dymock

LIFE AT WORK

Work is a huge part of our daily lives but many of our contributors highlighted that their day was filled with more than the work itself; the banter, friendship, socialising at lunchtimes and after work, organising company sports teams, outings and trade union activities all contributed to a sense of community. This section looks at some common themes that were mentioned in the interviews.

"You were brought up that you went to work. You were brought up that as soon as you left school you went to work, you got a job."

Josie Stevens

Starting Work

John Heathcote

"Well, my dad being a lorry driver and my mum working in a laundry, they were adamant that I had to get a trade, that I had to get an apprenticeship, I had to get a qualification, because they had never got a qualification. And I went to Manor Park Technical High School as it was then, and I got five or six O Levels, didn't go for A Levels because in those days I had no chance of going to university because my mum and dad couldn't afford it. But I went all out to get an apprenticeship…And a job came along at Clarkson's. They were looking for somebody with chemistry, physics, good technical qualifications to do metallurgy. At that point in time I didn't even know what metallurgy was, what it was all about. But I went for an interview with the works manager then, Mr Dennis Barker, nice old bloke. And he asked me some of the most awkward questions about gears on a bike, how they work…and I just kept saying, 'I don't know, I don't know.' And I was most surprised after a few weeks he said, "come for another interview, we want to see you again". And I said to him, 'Well, I couldn't answer the questions.' And he said, "But you were the only one who told me the truth…you just said you didn't know. I want someone honest like that." And they told me all about the job. It was going to be a five year apprenticeship, and I'd a chance to go to "the Butts" [Coventry Technical College] in Coventry, and then if I got my ONC in metallurgy I'd go on to Lanchester Polytechnic which is now Coventry University, and follow it on with an HNC, so I just threw myself into it. And looking back now on my lifetime, that qualification, that apprenticeship enabled me to go to South Africa, I had several good jobs in South Africa based on my UK qualifications…There were times when I hated on a Friday night to go to Lanchester Polytechnic, when all my mates were going down to the pub for a couple of pints, but I just had to bite the bullet and get on and pass my exams… I'm really proud of the fact that I did my apprenticeship, thanks to my mum and dad. They made me do it."

John Heathcote

Trade Unions

Trade unions were important in the workplace and beyond, providing advice and representation as well as community facilities and training for their members.

Ron Marston

Ron Marston worked at Armstrong-Siddeley and Intalok. At Intalok, he became involved in trade unionism and later became an area official for the Transport and General Workers Union (TGWU). Ron now runs the TGWU's retired members' group which provided a number of the Working Lives interviewees.

"Well the places where we had membership was in the main employers in Nuneaton; Sterling Metals…Intalok. And Courtaulds in textile industry, Union Wool and Leather which was a tannery, Fielding and Johnson's…, Lister's which was the carpeting company whose parent company were ICI. We had Clarkson's engineering tools, we had the hospitals, we had the local authority and then we had smaller companies such as Premier Stone that used to make concrete slabs up at Chapel End on what they used to call the old Dry Bread pit site…and, Biddles engineering, that was part of our membership. If you're talking about Bedworth…we had large pockets of membership at Bayton Road as well, Abbey Panels and places like that. So we had a large membership in this area. Cause when you think about it, Sterling were employing about two thousand and we were the major union. Intalok were employing nearly a thousand and we were the only union virtually there, there were just odd individuals in other unions. And Courtaulds, a thousand workers at one time when I was the official. And Clarkson's they had three hundred to four hundred people. Quite an industrial town and the T and G had a large membership here..

Well, I mean we had the convalescent homes…We used to have a sickness benefit and a funeral benefit, all of those that were far more an important factor in those earlier days than what they are now because the state has took over a lot of these functions. And of course then we'd pursue where people had accidents, and pursue a claim against the employer for neglect.
It also produced social activities because for instance if you took the Sterling Metals, they had three branches there, no four because the staff had a branch … so there was the social aspect as well which was all important to keeping people together."
Ron Marston, Transport and General Workers' Union

"We had us ups and downs. The biggest strike was for seven weeks I think. I can't even remember what it were about now! Money or conditions obviously…But there weren't many strikes really."

John Smith, Clarkson's

"I was out of work on occasions, but I was shop steward…I was the branch secretary of our union, which went against you. I lost a lot of jobs through that. When there was any redundancy list the steward would always be the one that was the first to go. That's one of the reasons I was in and out of work a lot really."

Geoff Elliott, sheet metal worker

"We used to pay a shilling a week union. Whatever I got out of it I don't know. Because everybody else paid it so we paid it so. They used to say, 'They're getting you rises,' and I thought, 'Well it's taking a long while to get the rise."

Eve Everitt on union membership at Hart and Levy

Ron Marston talks about his first taste of an industrial dispute at Intalok, which made springs for car seats and was on the site of the present Liquid and Envy nightclub.

"The majority (of workers) were women…and the women worked hard there, they did jobs such as on the machines that coiled the springs… And then they had another section where they put loops onto the springs….all hard on the women's hands…And also they had welding sections where the women worked. But what happened was that because of the demand for components at that time, the management brought in a professional company to advise them….And they came and brought their stopwatches and their boards and started observing. And course, there was this feeling, 'Huh, we work hard enough now without having these people watching us and timing us.' And course the word was said, 'Oh we ought to form a union,' "Ah they won't have a union here, they wouldn't recognise it, we've tried before." So we set about getting people into membership… These were ordinary working women. Good genuine women, most of them with families, who after working eight hours had got to go home and look after the children and provide the meals at home etc. And they were good workers.

So consequently this caused quite some natural agitation amongst the women. And plus they were saying to me, "What's the union going to do about it?" Well, the union had wrote to the company for recognition and the company hadn't responded to the correspondence. In later life I came across this a lot but this was my first taste of it. And so the women of their own accord, no ballot, no nothing, stopped work…so I went out the factory and rang the union organiser in Coventry and told him the situation. So he said, 'Right, go back into the factory and tell the girls not to start work until the management agree to meet me.'

And these women weren't versed in union practices. They were probably daughters and sisters of trade unionists in other places but they hadn't been accustomed to trade union practices themselves."
Ron Marston

The hatting industry had its own unique way of resolving disputes amongst the workers.
Fred Arkinstall, Hall and Phillips' hat factory

"I was a bit nervous about whether I ought to tell you this because we, some of the things you were not allowed to discuss or it was a bit taboo at the time… But they didn't have a union there,

Visit by Duke of Windsor to Hall and Phillips' hat factory 1934. Courtesy of Warwickshire Library and Information Service.

no union. But in that finishing shop they had a way of doing things like, if you, if somebody annoyed you in any way, if somebody just, if you were working on a particular job and you put your brush down and they decide to be a bit silly and take it away.

… You had a special procedure that you went to this man, I want you to be careful and underline this, and you went to him and you say, 'Is your name Johnny Smith, shop mate of mine?' And he'd say, "Yes." 'I shall insist that you pay a shilling for annoyance.' And the other thing about that was your shop steward then was what they called the 'bobby of the week' and the journeymen took it in turns to be the bobby. And it was the bobby's job then to come and ask this man if he'd give his word, he'd paid the shilling for annoyance and he'd paid this money."

Women at Work

"I tell you the truth I loved to work. I never worked in Africa but when I start I really enjoyed...I was independent from since I come in England."

Kokab Jahan Choudury

Kokab Jahan Choudury

Mrs Kokab Jahan Choudury worked as a machinist at Abbey Hosiery in Nuneaton. She moved from Kenya to the UK in 1971, and talks about how this gave her a new opportunity to work and become more independent. She also had to care for her husband when he became ill.

"I started off in the typing pool. I think there was about twelve of us if I remember rightly in just one great big room. We typed invoices, letters. If any of the secretaries were out we had to go and take down in shorthand and type it then... And we used to have to go through the factory to the office in the factory to pick bits up and I hated that, used to hate that...because it was all blokes and I mean I was a naïve girl of nineteen, and all blokes, and they just all used to stand and stare you know all the work seemed to stop when a woman walked through. And the noise, and the smell of the grease. Yes, very eye-opening it was. Brought me out of myself a bit, it did. Made me a bit more confident than I was when I started work." Patricia Carbutt

Patricia Carbutt

Patricia Carbutt, a secretary at Clarkson's engineering, describes what it was like being one of only a few women in a male environment.

Avis Keal worked in a number of engineering firms on the shop floor, and talked about inequality of pay, and how it felt to be paid a lower rate for the same job.

Courtesy of Avis Keal

Many women left work when they got married or when they had children. This break in their working life could lead to a loss of confidence about returning to work, or could provide the impetus for a change.

"It was only after my eldest was born that I decided that I need to do something with my life… because if I don't do it now I'm never going to get the chance to do it. And because I always had that at the back of my mind, anyway, that when I left school I never was given the opportunity to explore different career options or to do further studies. I took the opportunity, and my husband supported me fully…of going out to the college one day and just asking about what career options there were out there for me. I started off by doing a couple of assertive skills course just to get my confidence back and this job, what I'm doing now, which is a care assistant for Social Services that came up."
Farida Sheikh

"It was when I went to the Dunlop…The job that I was on, men did come and work on it, there was one in particular who was on it regular as well and he got a male rate and you got a female rate. As a matter of fact you could actually have a batch of work and you'd got to get that batch of work out so they would put you on together and he would do his job identical to you and he'd get paid twice as much…It got up your nose a bit, but even though I was getting half the price of what a male was getting, it was still better pay than a lot of the other firms.

(At the Dunlop) A lot of the inspection was [done by] females…but they gradually got rid of them and on all the other jobs they gradually got rid of the women…Well, they worked you out…I was one of the last females on that machine shop floor." *Avis Keal*

Commuting

Many people travelled to Hinckley to work in the hosiery factories or to Coventry's large engineering works. By 1931, 1200 workers a day were travelling from Nuneaton to Coventry to work, and by 1951 this figure had increased to over 9000.

Eileen Jacobs was one of many Nuneaton girls that worked in the hosiery factories of Hinckley. Paid on piecework, she used to earn more money than her father did as a miner. She used to cycle there and back, sometimes twice a day, coming home at lunchtime to check if she had a letter from her future husband who was serving in the army during the Second World War.

"I went to Hinckley, in the hosiery and I think it was about half a crown a week on the bus and I wanted a bike. So my dad signed for me to have a bike on the hit and miss as they called it then. And the half a crown a week that was my bus fare was paid on the bike…so I used to bike to work…

Whatever it come, rain or shine I used to cycle. And if I got caught out coming home I used to wrap some brown paper round my legs to keep them dry …

[The journey took] twenty minutes… depending on the wind, if the wind was facing you it was harder you see, but if the wind was behind you it was all right."

Eileen Jacobs

Cycling in Queen's Road, 1945.
Courtesy of Warwickshire Library and Information Service.

Fun and Games

In Nuneaton and Bedworth in the second part of the 20th Century, there were many large firms that provided a sports and social club for their workers, even dance halls in the case of Courtaulds and Sterling Metals.

"They used to have their own social club. They used to have one of the best dancefloors in town, Stermet Hall…We used to have some good dances there… used to have all the big bands there, Sid Lawrence and all those."

Bill Baker, Sterling Metals

The Stermet Hall was a canteen during the day:

"The canteen which used to be at Stermet Hall…you'd probably have 2000 people going in there for meals in the day. And then you used to have the bar upstairs which was just as busy. We used to go up in our break. We used to have an hour at one time so by time you ate your sandwiches, say 'oh we'll go up and have a game of table tennis' or…we used to go over and have a game of football but we were always late coming back because you used to play until you heard the buzzer go. Well the buzzer went at three minutes to one and you'd got to be back at one o'clock…so you'd see about 30 or 40 blokes jumping the brook and all dashing across the road getting to work to clock on. Otherwise you used to lose quarter of an hour if you were two minutes over."

Bill Baker, Sterling Metals

"We used to have an old lady in the canteen and she used to send up to George's bakery for some new bread and slice it about two inches thick and cover it in treacle and the girls used to go mad for it! 'Cause the bread was hot, it used to make the treacle run and we always used to have that for our breakfast."

Eve Everitt, Hart and Levy

**Canteen ladies at the Union Wool and Leather Company, 1980's.
Courtesy of Ron Baldwin.**

"I enjoyed my time there because as I say you got all sport and everything. Used to pay a penny a week for that, taken out of your salary. And you got all the hockey kit and everything, you never had to pay for any of it. They used to pay for pads, sticks, teas for entertaining the other side, it was good. And I played tennis as well. …Up at the Dunlop sports field they had got a hard court…they were pretty well equipped…I played table tennis as well sometimes…And I was a member of the Drama Society at the Dunlop."

Angela Woodcock, Dunlop Wheel and Rim Company

John Hopkins recalls that although the quarry football team no longer existed when he worked there, there were other hobbies that many quarrymen enjoyed.

"The main thing that held them together quite a few of them used to go fishing together…They certainly started me off when I was young. In the canal…used to live down there in the summer."

John Hopkins, Judkins' quarry

Judkins' quarry circa 1980. On the left is Martin Hotchkiss, Senior Technician and right is Technician John Small enjoying a dinnertime game of chess. Courtesy of Mick Russell.

"We'd go down the Co-op Hall, you know where the Kwik Save is now… I saw the Silver Beatles, the Beatles when they were the Silver Beatles, I saw the Stones on a Friday night…It used to be about five bob on a Friday night. And we used to go in the Nag's Head first, have a couple of pints, then go up to the Co-op Hall Friday night and Saturday night. That was it, that was the Mecca for all the young people, the Co-op Hall."

John Heathcote

Some companies supported works sports teams.

"The sheet metal workers had a football team, we had cricket, we had bowls, we had snooker, darts… I went to Joe Chinn when I was sixteen, I said, 'Mr Chinn we'd like a cricket team' I said 'but… we ain't got no gear', "I'll buy the stuff", he was very brass, "you'd better bloody win summat."

Geoff Elliott, sheet metal worker

This is Avis Keal and some of her colleagues from Kenning's (later Toye, Kenning & Spencer) on a works day out to Skegness in the late 1940's. Back (L-R): Avis Keal, unknown; front (L-R): unknown, Christine ? Courtesy of Avis Keal.

Wartime Memories

Factories were requisitioned for war work during the Second World War. Arthur Brittain describes how the Haunchwood Brick and Tile Co Ltd's brick kilns were used.

"They transferred us down to Five Yard that were down Bermuda. 'Cause you've heard of the blue lagoon haven't you? Well that clay hole there we were the last ones to work that, up there…in 1941… And then we stopped making blue bricks and all that and they used the kilns and we used to do bomb case hardenings. And you know the tanks, the tracks…we used to harden them. We used to put them in saggars like and we used to put these in and they used to put iron ore in and put them in the kilns and they used to burn them for so long…And they used to have to keep it at constant heat for about four days. We were doing these tram tracks and before you put them in, if you hit them with a hammer they'd snap… But after they'd been through this process you could hit them with a blooming sledgehammer and you wouldn't dent them nor nothing."
Arthur Brittain

"You see a lot of the girls and young women that worked there, their husbands and boyfriends were all in the forces then…Some of them used to sew their names and addresses in the pockets of the trousers and there was a lot of Canadian officers that wrote to some of them. But I daren't do nothing like that. I weren't old enough. But you had to grow up well when you was in factories, believe me."

Eve Everitt, Hart and Levy

Market Square, Nuneaton 1940's. Countesy of Warwickshire Library and Information Service.

"See the older people went into munitions and they were glad of the younger ones to do these jobs (garment making). It was war work but it weren't so well paid as the munitions so of course we dropped into these jobs…"

Eve Everitt

Finishing
Work

"I enjoyed my job, I really did. In fact, when I retired, they come down for me twice to go back."

Mary Spicer, Sterling Metals

"I think basically until you lose your job you don't know how happy you were in it until you go and do another one. I mean things out there are getting a sight worse than they used to be…It gets you down. It really gets depressing when you're not getting the information, and everything's kept in the dark. You know there's something wrong but you don't know what's wrong…especially after that length of service like. Because the older you get the less chance of you getting another job. But I did."

John Smith, Clarkson's

"I enjoyed it at Abbey Hosiery, I enjoyed it at Kenning's, but I've also enjoyed being at home. Because you've always got so many things to do."

Margaret Dewis

Conclusion

Brick and tile making, quarrying, textiles and engineering all shaped Nuneaton and Bedworth throughout the 19th and 20th centuries.

Much of the work in the extractive and manufacturing industries was labour intensive and required large workforces. These large factories have now all but disappeared, and with them the shared sense of camaraderie and community.

Factories and industrial sites were also a visible part of the towns' landscape, good or bad. Now, these local landmarks have gone. Modern industry is now tucked away into dedicated industrial estates, such as Bayton Road in Bedworth.

There is still industry here but its face has changed. Manufacturing and engineering continue to be important industries in Nuneaton

Embroidery at Toye, Kenning & Spencer. Courtesy of Toye, Kenning & Spencer.

and Bedworth, but on a much smaller scale.

There are also some survivors of an earlier age. In Bedworth, Toye, Kenning & Spencer's Jacquard looms still clatter away making ribbons and regalia as they have done for many years, but now they also use computers to design new products.

Design work at Toye, Kenning & Spencer in 2008. Courtesy of Warwickshire Library and Information Service.

This project has captured a snapshot of work and industry in the 20th century and we hope it has given you an insight into the day to day life of working people in Nuneaton and Bedworth. With this book there is an audio CD which has soundscapes of the interviews. If you would like to hear more of the voices of the people who generously shared these memories with us, please visit the project website to listen to the full interviews.

www.warwickshire.gov.uk/workinglives

Access to the internet is available at any Warwickshire Library.

Bayton Road Industrial Estate, 2008. Courtesy of Warwickshire Library and Information Service.

List of Interviewees

Thank you to everyone who agreed to be interviewed

Unfortunately we could not include all the interviews in this booklet, so here is a list of all the participants.
All of these interviews are available to listen to on the website at **www.warwickshire.gov.uk/workinglives**

WL1	John Heathcote; Clarkson Engineers Ltd
WL2	Edward Jephcote, Jack Pallett; Stanley Brothers Ltd, Haunchwood Brick & Tile Co Ltd, Courtaulds Ltd, Coventry Climax Engineers Ltd
WL3	Josie Stevens; Lester and Harris Ltd, Fairbrothers F.N, Lister & Co Ltd, Fielding and Johnson Ltd, Toye, Kenning and Spencer Ltd, 3M UK Plc (Atherstone), Courtaulds Ltd
WL4	Abdul Qauym Din; British Rail Ltd
WL5	Kokab Jahan Choudury; Abbey Hosiery Mills Ltd, Thorn Lighting
WL6	Zainub Kapadia; Abbey Hosiery Mills Ltd, High End Fashion
WL7	Mr Ebrahim (surname anonymous); Fielding and Johnson Ltd, Courtaulds Ltd, Sterling Metals Ltd
WL8	Raymond Coles; Midland Quarry Co Ltd, Boons Granite Quarry Ltd, Jees Hartshill Granite & Brick Co Ltd, Standard Plutech, Scotts of Hinckley
WL9	Ronald Baldwin; Webster and Bennett Ltd, Union Wool and Leather Co Ltd
WL10	Farida Sheikh; Abbey Hosiery Mills Ltd
WL11	Sharifa Khalifa; Abbey Hosiery Mills Ltd, Courtauld's Ltd, Multi Textiles
WL12	Farida Skingley; Nortex, Sartex
WL13	Jenab Chhibu; Abbey Hosiery Mills Ltd
WL14	Mihraj Begum; Lorat
WL15	Anonymous, Abbey Hosiery Mills Ltd; Courtaulds Ltd, Supreme Hosiery Co Ltd
WL16	Mumtaz Mughal; self-employed caterer
WL17	Saeeda Qureshi; self-employed caterer
WL18	Alan Green; Fielding and Johnson Ltd, Rufus Jones & Son, Lister & Co Ltd, British Coal (Baddesley Pit)
WL19	Peter Hornsby; Haunchwood Brick and Tile Co Ltd, Fielding and Johnson Ltd
WL20	Anonymous; Reliable Clothing Co Ltd, Hart and Levy Ltd, Lister & Co Ltd, Fielding and Johnson Ltd
WL21	John Smith; Clarkson Engineers Ltd, Haunchwood Colliery
WL22	Geoff Elliott; Chinns Engineering Ltd, Abbey Panels Ltd, Rolls Royce Plc, Jaguar Cars Ltd, Car Panels, Letchford Swift Motor Panel Co Ltd Motor Panel Co Ltd, Park Sheet Metal Co Ltd, Armstrong Whitworth Aircraft Co Ltd, Whitworth-Gloucester Aircraft Ltd
WL23	Ron Marston; Armstrong Siddeley, Intalok Ltd, Transport and General Workers' Union
WL24	Mary Spicer; Sterling Metals Ltd

WL25	Roy Dymock; S and F Engineering Ltd, Armstrong Whitworth Aircraft Co Ltd, Riley (Coventry) Ltd, Coventry Art Castings Co Ltd
WL26	Evelyn Everitt; Hart and Levy Ltd, Conner, Alfred & Co Ltd, Dunlop Co Ltd
WL27	Fred Stevens; William Moorhouse and Sons Ltd, British Thompson Houston Ltd (BTH), Coventry, Clarkson Engineers Ltd, Dunlop Co Ltd, Armstrong Whitworth Aircraft, Massey Ferguson Ltd
WL28	William Baker; Sterling Metals Ltd
WL29	Arthur Brittain; Stanley Brothers Ltd
WL30	Frederick Arkinstall; Hall and Phillips Ltd
WL31	Ian Cartwright; Midland Sheet Metal Works Ltd, ABJ Engineering, Atherstone, Alec Rule Mechanical Handling, Lloyd's School of Welding, British Trance Co Ltd
WL32	Ronald Smith; British Trane Co (Biddles)
WL33	Marian Garside; school teacher. Her father worked at Stanley Brothers Ltd
WL34	Sheila Moore; Co-operative Dairy, her parents worked at Stanley Brothers Ltd
WL35	Dennis Lovatt; Sanderson & Son Engineering; Cavall Tools
WL36	Angela Woodcock; Reliable Clothing Company, Dunlop Co Ltd
WL37	Joe Craner; Grant's (Coventry), Franklin's, Kenning's (later Toye, Kenning & Spencer Ltd)
WL38	Reginald Brandist; London Brick Co, Marston Hall Depot, Bedworth, Shuresta (A. Mirecki) Ltd, Bayton Road, Bedworth
WL39	John Hopkins; Judkins Ltd, Jaguar Cars Ltd
WL40	Douglas Watson; Dunlop Co Ltd, his father was quarry manager at Charles Abell Quarry
WL41	Raymond Clay; Haunchwood Brick and Tile Ltd (Bermuda), Courtauld Ltd (Coventry)
WL42	Percy Rogers; Arley Colliery Co Ltd, Abbey Panels Ltd
WL43	Patricia Carbutt; Clarkson Engineers Ltd
WL44	Avis Keal; Kennings, Toye Kenning & Spencer Ltd, GEC; Alfred Herbert Limited, Shuresta (A. Mirecki) Ltd, Bedworth, Dunlop Co Ltd
WL45	Eileen Jacobs; Gent's Hosiery (Hinckley) Dunlop Co Ltd
WL46	Frank Jacobs; Courtauld Ltd
WL47	Margaret Dewis; Abbey Hosiery Mills Ltd, Toye, Kenning & Spencer Ltd
WL48	Trevor Moreton; Courtauld Ltd, Arley Colliery, Coventry Colliery (Keresley), National Coal Board
WL49	Roy Jennings; Haunchwood Brick and Tile Co Ltd
WL50	Jonah Moore; Co-operative Society Ltd (Dairy)
WL51	Eric Byewater; Midland Sheet Metal Works Ltd
WL52	Joan Beresford; Courtaulds Ltd
WL53	Robert Jackson; Arley Colliery
WL54	Clifford Ginns; Midland Sheet Metal Works Ltd

WL1-WL51 were conducted and recorded by Alison Clague, assisted by Les Holmes.

WL52-54 were conducted and recorded by Les Holmes and Robert Sloan, circa 1996. These analogue recordings were digitised for the Working Lives Project.

Glossary

Textiles

Altered the "twists" on the machine The amount of 'twist' in yarn can change the strength, smoothness, and uniformity of yarn.

Anthony Eden hat A widely used name for a type of man's silk-brimmed, black felt Homburg hat. The style was favoured in the 1930's by Anthony Eden, a politician who later became Prime Minister in the years 1955-57.

Bobbin A spool or reel that holds thread or yarn for spinning, weaving or knitting.

Bobbin boy Someone who transported bobbins from the mules to be weighed and cleaned.

Bowler hat The bowler hat (also known as a 'derby' or 'billycock') is a hard felt hat with a rounded crown. Traditionally worn by 'city gents'.

"Changed the belts" A system of leather belts and pulleys supplied power to looms or other machinery. The belts would sometimes slip off the pulley wheel which sent the power to the loom and would need to be put back on. This was very dangerous to do when the wheels were still spinning.

Creeler A textile worker who tends the creel which holds bobbins of yarn to ensure a continuous supply of yarn.

Cutter A worker who cuts out shapes from fabric which will be sewn together to make clothing.

Dye sheds An area in a textile factory where yarn or fabric is dyed.

Fez A red felt hat in the shape of a truncated cone with a tassle of Turkish origin.

Foreman/foremistress/ foremiss Someone who supervises a group of workers and manages their work.

Handfinisher A worker who adds the finishing touches to garments by hand, for example adding buttons.

Jacquard loom A mechanical loom, invented by Joseph Marie Jacquard in 1801. It can produce very detailed woven designs using a system of sheets of cardboard punched with holes. Each row of holes corresponds to one row of the design. Many rows of holes are punched on each card and the many cards that compose the design of the textile can be strung together. Each hole in the card controls a hook, which can either be up or down. The hook raises or lowers the warp thread so that the weft will either lie above or below it to create the pattern.

Journeyman Someone who has completed an apprenticeship in a trade.

Loom A device for weaving thread or yarn together to make fabric. The most basic loom is a frame which holds the upright or warp threads under tension so that threads (the weft) can be woven through them with a shuttle.

Mule room A mule is a large multi-spindle spinning machine that make fibres into yarn. A mule room is an area in a textile factory where this type of machinery is housed.

Narrow weaving Weaving narrow fabrics like ribbons, elastic and webbing.

Outworker Workers who were based outside the factory, taking in work to do at home. It would usually be delivered to them and then collected when complete.

Pick A weft thread in a fabric.

Piece work A system where you are paid by how many items you make, so the faster you work, the more you are paid.

Quality control A procedure to check the quality of production to ensure it meets set standards.

Reeler A worker that tends textile machinery that winds yarn.

Shuttle A device used with a loom that carries the weft thread back and forth between the threads of the warp to weave fabric.

Steam presses Large machines

used to press fabric and garments to remove creases.

Tannery A place where animal skins are processed to turn them into leather.

Trilby hat A soft felt hat with a narrow brim and a deeply indented crown. Worn by men in the twentieth century.

Twelve and six /eighteen and six These phrases refer to pre-decimal money. Decimilisation was introduced in1971. Twelve and six was equivalent to 62.5 new pence and eighteen and six equivalent to 92.5 pence.

Velour A velvet-like fabric

Warp thread - see 'Loom'.

Weft thread - see 'Loom'.

Winding Making bobbins of yarn.

Quarrying

Ballast Crushed stone used as a bed for railway tracks. Also/or stone used as ballast on ships, to provide extra weight.

Crusher Large machinery that crushes up stone to different sizes for different uses.

Detonator A device used to set off an explosion.

Landfill site A place where rubbish is put into a large hole in the ground to be buried. Often old quarry sites are used for this purpose.

Quarry face The part of the quarry that is being worked.

Shot-firing Using explosives to break up the stone in the quarry.

Wharf A landing area where goods can be loaded and unloaded onto canal boats.

Brickyards

Airbrick A brick with ventilation holes.

Blue yard A brickyard producing blue bricks rather than red bricks.

Bullnose bricks A type of brick with a rounded edge. Available as single or double bullnose.

Endless rope haulage A rope which has its two ends spliced together and is driven by passing over a friction wheel which in turn is driven by a motor. The tubs are fixed to the rope which pulls them along rails.

Fettling Removing excess clay from the seams and edges of a moulded chimneypot before it is fired.

Gang A group of people working together to do a particular task.

Piece work A system where you are paid by how many items you make, so the faster you work, the more you are paid.

Kiln A large brick built industrial oven.

Saggars Containers made of fireclay which are used to enclose pots and protect them from the flames, smoke and gases in the kiln.

Tippling Tubs containing clay or other material using a tippler to empty them.

Engineering

Alloy A metallic substance which is composed of two or more chemical elements of which at least one is a metal. Different mixtures have different properties.

Blocking hammer A type of hammer used to shape sheet metal.

Capstan lathe A machine used to make shaped metal objects.

Cobalt A hard silver-grey metal, that is used in the preparation of magnetic and high-strength alloys.

Cutting tools Used in engineering. The part of a machine tool which comes into contact with, and removes material from the workpiece by the use of a cutting medium. Also known as a cutter.

Chuck/universal chuck A device that affixes to a mill, lathe or drill-press spindle. It holds a tool or workpiece by one end, allowing it to be rotated.

Die shop Where a casting process takes place. Molten metal is forced under high pressure into the cavity of a metal mould.

Dollies A dolly is a shaped piece of metal, like a small handheld anvil, used with a hammer to shape sheet metal.

Fettling Removing excess metal from a casting. Processes such as grinding, chipping and shot blasting are used.

Labour pool A group of workers who could be called on to do a variety of jobs.

Lathe A tool designed for precisely machining hard materials. It removes material from a rotating object by movements of various cutting tools, such as tool bits and drill bits.

Metallurgical Metallurgy is the scientific study of metals and their alloys. In engineering, knowledge of metallurgy is used to achieve a balance between material properties such as cost, weight, strength, toughness, hardness and corrosion resistance, and performance by methods including production of alloys, shaping, heat treatment and surface treatment of the product.

Milling A machining operation where metal or other material is removed by applying power to a rotating cutter.

Munitions Military supplies, especially weapons and ammunition.

Planishing hammer A flat faced hammer used to smooth dents.

Shop boy Before becoming an apprentice, new employees may have to run errands and prove themselves capable of being good workers. At Midland Sheet Metal Works this role was referred to as the Shop Boy.

Snips A tool used to cut sheet metal.

Tail fin Part of an aeroplane or a bomb designed to fly through the air.

Turning A way of removing material from a rotating workpiece, usually with a single-point cutting tool in a lathe.

Welding A fabrication process that joins metal by melting the work pieces and adding a filler material to form a pool of molten material that cools to become a strong joint.

Wheeling A technique to shape sheet metal into curved three-dimensional shapes, for example to form car body panels. A Wheeling Machine or English Wheel is a device made up of an upper and lower wheel, the sheet metal being moved between them.

Bibliography

Cook, Alan. *Extractive Industry of the Nuneaton Area; A History of Man's Use of Stone 100,000 BC to 2001AD,* [vol.7] (Nuneaton: Home Piece, 2000)

Field, Paul and Press, Mike. *The Top Sixty: A Study of the Sixty Largest Employers in Nuneaton and Bedworth.* [Prepared by Research Partnership] (Nuneaton: Planning and Development Department of Nuneaton and Bedworth Borough Council, 1988)

Milburn, Dennis. *Nuneaton; the Growth of a Town.* (Nuneaton: Nuneaton Corporation Library & Museum Committee, 1963)

Nuneaton Society Newsletters; edited by Peter Lee. [Nuneaton: Nuneaton Society, 1989-]

Veasey, E.A. *Nuneaton; A History.* (Stroud: Phillimore & Co Ltd, 2002)

All available at Nuneaton Library, Warwickshire Library and Information Service.

For details visit: **www.warwickshire.gov.uk/librarycatalogue**

All photographs unless otherwise stated are from the Local Studies Illustration Collection at Nuneaton Library.

Index of People and Companies